Whistling Girls and Crowing Hens

Joy E. Ingram

ISBN 978-1-64515-122-7 (paperback)
ISBN 978-1-64515-226-2 (hardcover)
ISBN 978-1-64515-123-4 (digital)

Christian Faith Publishing, Inc.
832 Park Avenue
Meadville, PA 16335
www.christianfaithpublishing.com

Printed in the United States of America

To my husband, Anthony. I would like to thank him for his love and constant support and gentle prodding to finish this work. To my two children: my daughter, Michelle, and my son, Aaron. It is my sincere desire that they also will keep the legacy of storytelling alive.

Acknowledgements

I have often said, "Everyone needs at least one black mama." I am thankful for my black mama. Some people learn their history in school by reading and doing research. Although I have a master's degree in history, I thank my mother for passing this rich legacy on to me. I also want to thank my Aunt Edna, Grandmamma Georgia, cousin Sandy, Aunt Cora, Sally T., cousin Willie, cousin C. Bose, Miss Tommie, cousin Bessie, cousin Geraldine, Momma Lula Ingram, Charlotte Ingram, and all my other hosts of black mamas and female relatives who have been the source of countless inspiration for this book.

I want to thank my sister Marion DeVelle Contini for always, always being there for me in ways that even she is not aware. I want to thank my sister BJ Patrick for being my biggest cheerleader and constantly keeping a fire under me to write and tell the story of this remarkable human being that gave us life.

My pastors Dr. Ed and Nora King, and my Redemption Church Family.

My niece Keva DeVelle Horry for going before me and publishing a book.

I would like to thank Ronni Chandler and everyone through the years that knew Miss Mamie and shared with me their own mother's wit.

I would like to thank my friend and colleague Dr. Toni McDaniel for always encouraging me to tell my story.

I want to thank my girls Darleen Weigel, Shiela Whitaker, Kathy Richards, Yvonne Wilson, Lori Lennon, Lisa "Leera" Orr, Wendy Boyd, and Tiffanny Greenlee.

I want to thank Gabby Wenger for keeping me laughing and encouraging me to finish this book.

I want to thank my good friend Rachel Reed for inspiring me in too many ways to mention.

Introduction

You may have heard that actions speak louder than words. This is very true. But for myself and for many others, the words and phrases that we grew up with as children have influenced our actions and therefore ring very loudly in our lives. I grew up on a rich diet of words and phrases that shaped and molded me into my adulthood and even until today. You see, I did not grow up influenced by the writings of Voltaire or the paintings of Rembrandt, but I grew up on the words and phrases of a little black Southern woman with a man's middle name—Floyd. She hailed from Elberton, Georgia. She barely had an elementary school education but was one of the wisest women I have ever had the privilege of knowing. She barely stood five feet tall. She flashed a big pretty smile for anyone who came to call on her, and her perfect white teeth (as she proudly proclaimed to anyone she first met, "You know I got all my teeth") were a sharp contrast to her coffee-colored skin. As a matter of fact, us kids called her *Coffee* behind her back. My daddy's skin color defied the notion that he was a black man as he was as white as any Caucasian around.

Several years ago, I started recording and compiling the sayings of my mother as a sort of hobby. Much to my surprise, when I would use some of my mother's quips, other people, many of whom are colleagues of mine, would share with me some of the sayings of their mothers, aunts, grandmothers, etc. I began to notice that although many of the sayings were definitely unique, at the same time they had many similar qualities. No matter what city I travel to, especially in the South, I very seldom find another African American or Appalachian woman—at least of the baby-boomer era—that I do not have something in common with. Generally, this bond of commonality often comes from not just how we were raised but from the words on which we were raised. Many of us find that we share common practices after giving birth, common parenting skills, common views on dating, and a common outlook on the world that is generally influenced more by what has been deposited in us than by outside influences.

Why are these sayings so influential? What is it about them that make us not only cherish them but also pass them on to our sons and daughters? We tend to imitate our parents and pass on bits and pieces of our family history and traditions to our children. The passing on of sayings and witticisms is no exception, and I suppose is as old as civilization itself.

Far more important than the humor is the uncanny wisdom of these sayings. Through the years I have gained strength, found advice in relationships, been comforted, and otherwise been made a richer person for having been a recipient of this rich heritage.

I did not fully comprehend just how much these sayings had become internalized until I would often find myself unconsciously using the sayings and witticisms in my history lectures. I have often, over the years, been asked by my students concerning the origins of these sayings. When I stopped to reflect, I must admit my first recollections come from my grandmother who lived until the age of eighty-three. I can remember as a child going to my grandmother's house in Athens, Georgia, and spending hours upon hours listening to her as she stood on the porch of her little wooden house and performed for literally about thirty people that she had dubbed as her "yard children." They would gather at dusk from the neighborhood, and someone would bring Miss Georgia, as she was called, a chair. The interesting thing is that she very seldom would be seated but oftentimes found herself prancing back and forth telling stories and dishing out mother wit at will.

Wherever the source, many of these sayings were, in some cases, casually spoken. In other cases, they came as strong admonition as a result of or to prevent some undesirable action. Whatever the reasons, these sayings have become internalized as part of a rich family legacy, affecting our everyday lives in quiet unspoken ways. For example, to this day I can not whistle. It is certainly not because I am not physically able to whistle, but like many other African American women, I grew up believing that this was not only unladylike but could possibly affect the way I would turn out as an adult. I still feel the need to remain quiet and still during a thunderstorm. However, I no longer believe that if I giggle or make playful noises that God will strike me where I sit for being disrespectful. There is, nonetheless, still that deep awe and respect for God's handiwork.

I rarely, if ever, talked back to my parents, especially my mother. If I did not find myself in the "middle of next week" or "wake up dead," I knew I at least wanted to live past that day. It is funny. I don't believe anyone really knows where the place called the "middle of next week" is, but few have dared to do what it took to venture there. I am also very thankful for my taste buds. As a matter of fact, long before I studied science in grade school and found out exactly what and where taste buds are, I knew they had to be very special because Mama frequently threatened to slap them out of my mouth. Certainly, such threats today might be considered child abuse, at the very least cruel. I have never been abused, nor do I now consider myself the victim of cruelty but rather acknowledge that I am a better person today because of these sayings. You can no more separate me from the sayings as you can from the fact that I have my mother's smile and my father's feet. They are a part of me. In an age of jargon and political correctness, they are a refreshing oasis from which to draw from.

What I have attempted to do with this work is to share some of the sayings of my mother and those of many other African American mothers whose witticisms and proverbs have nurtured, sustained, corrected, guided, and entertained generations of daughters throughout the years.

Interspersed throughout this book will be sayings of my mother. All of the sayings that are attributed to my mother are noted with an asterisk; all the other sayings were very generously shared with me by colleagues and friends whom I have met through the years. I think you will agree that in an age of political correctness and entitlement, it is refreshing to hear someone express themselves and their opinion without fear of offending someone or hurting someone's feelings. In an attempt to pass this rich legacy on to my children and the children of so many others whose lives have been affected by black mama wit—I write this book.

***"Who yo people?"**

An Extraordinary Woman

Ms. Mamie Floyd Liggett was born December 2, 1912, to Georgia and Bob Callahan in Elberton, Georgia. In spite of having little more than an elementary education, she went on to get her GED and graduate from cosmetology school and ultimately go on to open Liggett's Beauty Shop—one of the first black-owned businesses of its kind in the small Roane County town of Kingston, Tennessee. Georgia-born and raised throughout her lifetime, she never lost her Georgia accent; and when the correct words or subject-verb agreement escaped her, she either butchered the correct word or, out of convenience, simply made up her own. Try correcting your ninety-five-year-old mother when the doctor increases her medication to five hundred milligrams, but she proudly announces that she is now getting five hundred "mammograms" a day. *Scripture* became "stripture," *shock absorbers* became "schock-a-sog-gas," *pretty* became "prery," and *children* became "chiren" or "chulun," depending on the type of mood she was in.

Miss Mamie brought twelve chiren into the world. As she liked to explain, she had three "crops of chiren." It was to her third and last crop that I was born—the youngest of twelve. In spite having little more than an elementary school education, she went on to get her GED and graduated from cosmetology school, which ultimately allowed her to open her beauty shop. I never knew this until later, but she shared with me her inner desire to become a nurse. But since she did not have the proper education, she figured the next best thing (plus, she got to wear a uniform) was becoming a beautician. She and my father, Reverend Orange Gilbert Liggett, would be successful in sending most of those twelve children to college—two to private high schools. At the time of her death, those twelve chiren had produced some twenty-something grandchildren and over forty-something great-grands. Before becoming a beautician, she worked as a maid and cooked and cleaned for various white families while having to come home and cook and clean for her own.

I would be amiss if I did not introduce Orange Gilbert to you. Known around town as Reverend Liggett or Liggett by the white folks, he was simply known as Daddy by Mama. They called each other Mama and Daddy to get her children by her first marriage to call him Daddy. Orange Gilbert was a hero in his own right. He was born in 1896 (I still find it hard to believe that my daddy was born two years before the Spanish-American War) and fought on the front lines (something most colored servicemen were not allowed to do). Twenty years her senior, Miss Mamie confided in me once that she married Daddy not so much because she was in love with him (according to Miss Mamie, "I never did like a yella man" (referring to my father's fair skin tone) but because she had recently gotten saved in a revival, and she thought he would help keep her straight. They grew to love each other very much and had over fifty years together until his death in 1978.

Funny, in all the years they were married, I only heard them argue about twice. What I remember the most are the late nights I would lie in my bed attempting to fall asleep while listening to the laughter that would come from their bedroom (they never had a door, go figure that one). I found that laughter comforting almost in the same way I would awake to hearing my daddy pray for each and every one of his children and grandchildren. He quietly slipped away at home on April 23, 1978 after a stroke left him paralyzed on one side. Mama was determined, as she had promised, to never put him away in a nursing home but instead had a hospital bed and bedside commode delivered to the home where she took care of him until he took his last breath.

On February 24, 2008, at the age of ninety-five, my mother, Ms. Mamie Floyd Liggett, would take her last breath. She was surrounded by three of her twelve children who were able to hold her hand, sing, and pray with her while she quietly and peacefully slipped away with a smile on her face—as she would say, to her heavenly reward.

What can be said about a woman whose very presence and persona was larger than life? Whose life span covered the last seventeen presidential administrations, the Great Depression, two world wars, the war in Korea, the war in Vietnam, and the current war on terrorism. Her life experiences included both the invention of television and the first moon landing. Growing up in the South, she was no stranger to segregation, Jim Crow, and even run-ins with the Klan.

As she liked to tell me, I used to be taller, but I have shrunk a bit. This woman was Ms. Mamie Floyd Liggett. Most of the townspeople who knew her simply knew her as Miss Mamie, Ms. Liggett, or Sister Liggett, if you were considered to be, as Ms. Mamie said, "one of the saints" (simple meaning: church folk).

Standing by her bedside and watching her ninety-eight-pound frame fight for every breath, it is hard to imagine that this little lady once drove through a Klan rally and broke it up when she recognized one of the men's shoes. It is hard to imagine her and her good friend Miss Helen (both on crutches for some foot ailment) going into the superintendent's office and demanding that the schools in Kingston be integrated. Miss Mamie knew that *Brown v. Board of Education* passed the year her youngest baby was born declared segregation illegal, and 1964 was long enough for all deliberate speed to have run its course.[1]

It is hard to imagine this frail little creature along with my father building a church building. Not simple getting a congregation together but literally digging the foundation and laying bricks and constructing the building with a little help from the locals. Both she and my father would go on to pastor the Kingston Church of God until their subsequent deaths. Mama pastored the church with one

1. *Brown vs. Board of Education*, a landmark Supreme Court decision ruled in 1954 that segregation in public schools was unconstitutional and stated that integration must take place "with all deliberate speed."

faithful member, Marcella Willis, until she passed the torch on to my sister Sue.

She worked as a maid and took care of other people's children so she could make a better life for her children. She would cook and clean for them then come home to cook and clean for us.

It is hard to imagine this frail little creature running off almost every Jehovah's Witness that came by our house. Not physically running them off, but by the time she finished admonishing them about the error of their ways, they were usually in tears. As if this weren't enough, my father would generally finish the conversation while they ran by shouting, "I hope you see the error of your ways before it's finally everlasting too late, and you burn in a devil's hell."

It is hard to imagine her going in the backyard and running down a chicken or two and, with almost lightning-like precision, grabbing a strutting chicken, wringing its neck, and waiting for its headless body to quit running while spurting blood from its headless body and dropping so she could pluck it, gut it, clean, and cook it. I have always said, if Miss Mamie were left in the wilderness, she would do just fine. As a child, I thought she could move mountains and solve any problem (unless it were a math problem, of course). To say she was ambitious is an understatement. Her age never seemed to be a factor nor to slow her down. She drove up until the time that she was ninety-two (should not have been). She seemed to relish the idea of driving to the Walmart or to the Rite Aid. Although there were similar stores within a couple of blocks, she was adamant about getting on the interstate and driving to where she needed to go.

There was the incident when she was eighty-one and involved in a four-car pileup in which we suspect she did not see the traffic light change to green, for we would later find out she had cataracts. I will never forget walking with her inside her house where she was surprised to find out she had a red dress—she always thought it was green. Yikes is all I can still say.

Up until the time of her death in 2008 with stage four breast cancer, she always had a project going and was always looking forward to the next adventure. By the time we found out about her cancer, it had metastasized outside of her body and had begun to smell. She had hid this from her children for over two years as she knew she had strong faith in God to either heal or deliver her on earth or make her whole once she got to heaven. I will never forget one month before her passing, we—I should say my sister Sue—convinced her to go to the hospital to be checked as she was especially weak that night. It was a cold night in January, and when the doctors examined her, they were astounded to find she had been keeping her condition from us. They offered her morphine to cope with the pain. Her response was classic: "Honey, I've had twelve chiren [she was very proud to tell people this], and I wasn't a doper [drug addict] then, and you sho not go'n make a doper out of me now. Just brang me a li'l Tylenol, and I'll be fine."

I wanted to take the time to give you a brief introduction to this remarkable lady. It is only right that you should know something about her, for when she would meet someone for the first time, she would generally scrutinize them (although she became pretty good at not letting you know you were under major scrutiny). She would simply ask you, "Honey, who yo people?" and wait for your response. Now this saying on face value seems harmless enough; however, the simple translation in Miss Mamie's speech is, "You resemble someone I know. What do your parents do for a living? Who were their parents? Did they go to church? Are they good people?"

As a freshman in college, I met a guy named Spencer; we called him Spence. Now, you must admit, that is the most perfect name a handsome young man could have, and I desperately wanted to go out with Spence just to go bowling. By the time Miss Mamie dug around his family tree, she discovered his grandmother had owned a still several years ago, and that negated the deal. Needless to say, I never went out with Spence nor any other boys while I was at home. I will save those stories for my next book. If, in her myriad of questioning, she had decided she didn't like your pedigree or if you were a too-short male (she did not like short men, nor did she like her daughters dating them), she wouldn't fully shake your hand but rather offer you two limp fingers and a terse "hi do" then quickly walk away while you wondered what happened or if she called you by a wrong name. She was introduced to a Greg; she renamed and called him Paul. Such was Mamie Floyd.

More than her green thumb, more than her ability to stir up a "good ole pot of something," she was most proud of the fact as she liked to say in her down-home Georgia drawl. In spite of all that she accomplished in her ninety-five years, the one thing she would gladly tell any stranger in her down-home Southern Georgia accent was that, "I thank God for my salvation then," almost in the same breath without missing a beat proclaim, "And I thank God I got all ma teeth." For those of us who knew Miss Mamie, we each have our own story about what your first impression was upon meeting her. One would certainly be embraced by her broad warm smile as she flashed the gold filling in her mouth. We did not want her to get the gold, but the only dentist in town, who incidentally had one eye and was a member of the Klan, insisted on giving it to her. No matter what your impression was, you would eventually find out about her twelve chiren, as she referred to them always, but always a testimony about how good God is and always how she had all her teeth or could still touch her toes.

Her looks defied her ninety-five years of age. Before she became ill, it was not unheard of on any given Tuesday for her to be holding court in the Rite Aid, as she called it. "I'll give $20 to the person who can guess my age." She loudly and proudly proclaimed. "I'll buy lunch to anyone standing around here that can guess my age." Her eyes lit up as the light from an opening front door played against the gold in her mouth. Her slightly round frame shook with laughter and glee as numbers (all twenty years or more younger than her actual age) were called out. "Seventy-two," said one; "Fifty-five," said another; and so forth and so on. It's funny how she never let the game go on for more than a few minutes. Once she got her prescription or "scription," as she called it, from the pharmacist (who knew all too well her true age but seemed to be sworn to some unspoken oath of secrecy), she gathered up her belongings and walked away with the assurance that her $20 was secure.

***"A black man and a black car is just alike. They both look good, and they don't show they age easy."**

"Get In This House"

As kids, we were often sent outside to play especially in the summer. The only thing about going outside in the summer was the hot summer sun and the possibility of turning black. To us, that was a fate worse than death. No matter that my mother's dark-chocolate skin was the reason that she had earned the nickname *Coffee*, she could not stand the thought of us caramel- and peach-brown girls (well, actually, Sue was the only peach brown; I was what many would call paper-sack brown, and the rest a lighter to darker caramel). The necessary armor before being allowed to go outside in the summer was long sleeves (no matter how hot) and a large straw hat that shaded not only our faces but our tiny bodies as well. If one of use forgot to don the required summer armor, then we would hear a screeching yell, "Ah, Sue! Ah, Joy! Y'all get in this house from outside turning black."

At those words, we remembered, "Oh no," and started running full speed toward the closed screen door. Forgetting another crucial rule—"Shut that screen door fo the house gets full of flies"—we almost took the door off the hinges running side by side rather than one at a time through the door. We immediately and in panic started checking each other. If one did not know, they would have thought that we had just been exposed to toxic radiation as we immediately began to strip our clothes and check ourselves in the mirror. The questions came: "Oh no…am I black? Did I get dark?" Then Mama would echo, "I told yawl about going outside without a hat. Yawl just as black as can be!"

Many years have passed since those days of being sent outside with the "summer armor," but it is funny 'til this day. I still feel as if I am doing something wrong or, at the very least, forgetting something if I don't have a hat on and long sleeves when I go out in the sun. I no longer have the fear of turning black, but I still use plenty of sunscreen to protect my skin from damaging UV rays.

***"Drinking coffee will make you black."**

***"He sho ain't nobody'd pretty thang."**

***"You'll tie a knot with yo tongue that you can't untie with yo teeth (on getting married)."**

"Save a Sip Just for Me"

When I was a young girl about seven or eight, I would always love the smell of coffee. Really, the only coffee I ever smelled was that fixed by my mother coming from her percolator. You could hear it rumbling as if someone were trying to rev up a motor. Then *pluck, pluck, pluck*—I would watch as brown liquid bubbles filled the glass top. And as the bubbles disappeared, I knew the coffee was ready. I would watch my mother pour the liquid that adults only could drink into a cup, and she would hold the delicate small glass cup in one hand after sopping the last bite of toast into the cup. There was something about the way she would pull the last remaining goodness from the bottom of the cup that made me want to drink some. So that is what I did.

After she left the table, when no one was looking, I would double-back and finish her cup. This had become a daily ritual of mine for as long as I could remember. My secret, or so I thought. Little did I know at the time that Mama was leaving the small amount just for me. When Daddy found out, he tried to discourage me by saying it would stunt my growth or grow hair on my chest or some other such atrocity.

One day, while having breakfast and shortly before my ritual, Daddy called me over to the window to look. Lo and behold, it was Mr. Bill Jordan. Mama, with her Georgia accent, pronounced it *Jurdan*. Mama said, "Yon goes Bill Jurdan." For some reason, although we lived in the middle of town, Mr. Bill Jordan (as the kids were always required to address adults by *miss* or *mister* before saying their name) was driving a wagon pulled by an old mule. There he was. He sat high and tall on that wagon as black as my new black patent leather shoes. To my horror, my daddy told me that Bill Jordan used to be white, but he drank his momma's coffee, and now he's black. I gasped. Oh no. I thought, *I don't want to be black like Bill Jordan*. He furthermore told me that, that was why Mama was black. As I recall, the horror of turning black lasted only for about five minutes as I quietly slipped back into the dining room and slurped the last bit of coffee from Mama's cup.

***"A whistling girl and a crowing hen never come to no good end (on young ladies doing "unladylike" things)."**

Having raised mainly girls, there were certain things that we as young ladies were schooled in, and it goes without saying that we certainly understood our place both in the home and outside. I always knew not to interrupt when grown folks were talking; and if you knew what was right, you made yourself scarce and didn't make too many trips through a room where they were sitting. You knew to never ever address an adult by their first name. It was "Miss Mollie" or "Miss Pidd," Mr. "OD," "Miss Lady Mae," "Miss Big Ada." And even the town drunk, local abortionist, and brothel owner (yes, we had all three) were addressed with respect if you were a child.

I remember growing up in a family where you had to be quiet during a thunderstorm because, as Mama would always tell us, "the Lord is doing his handiwork." If we were watching TV, we had to turn off and unplug the TV (which gave us all three channels by the way), turn off all the lights (if they had not already been knocked out by electricity), and sit in quiet darkness until the storm subsided. For that reason even today, I find myself lowering my voice and getting quiet during a bad thunderstorm. I hated being still and quiet because they usually came in the middle of some fascinating adventure (going across country in a wagon train or fighting aliens from outer space) my sister Sue and I were about to embark on.

To this day, I do not know how to whistle and have a strong disdain when I hear other women do it successfully. I must admit, it would certainly come in handy when trying to get my stubborn hound dog Boaz's attention. As far back as I can remember, whenever I would even try to whistle, either Daddy or Mama would run toward me and say, "Honey, don't do that!" I would look more startled than puzzled and ask why. All I was trying to do was whistle along with the *Andy Griffith* theme song. "Becaause, chil', everybody knows that a whistling girl and a crowing hen never come to no good end." To this day, in spite of numerous attempts, I cannot whistle. Not even one note.

"A Hard Day's Night"

Summertime, for most people—well, not most of the people I knew and grew up with but most of my white friends—meant family-vacation time. I am sad to say that neither my family nor my parents ever went on a vacation. What summer meant for the Liggett family was no school but long hot days, plenty of housework or chores—whether it was washing dishes, ironing clothes in the cool of the day, for there was no air-conditioning (are you kidding me—what was that? Only window fans and a standing floor fan that we used as a pretend microphone when Mama and Daddy had left the house), snapping green beans, licking S&H Green Stamps, and picking grapes from the grape vine on the side of our yard once they were ripe.

At evening, about six o'clock was dinnertime. Dinnertime meant watching the Vietnam War on television or the civil rights marches. It mean chewing your food in silence as the television was turned loud enough to hear what the body count was. Daddy, always seated at the head of the table, had leaned his seat back just far enough to get a glimpse of something important. If it wasn't the body counts, it was what was going on with those "poor ole Negroes" in Selma, Alabama, or some other Southern town. I remember hating the news 'cause—as with thunderstorms—we always had to be quiet, and that meant not cutting up.

The fun part of summers was getting to stay up late on Sunday nights to watch *The Ed Sullivan Show*, walking to the local drugstore for a ten-cent cherry smash, and watching Mama frying fish or chicken in a kitchen that has to be over a thousand degrees. Yes, all were a part of my summers. Summers meant snapping green beans or going blackberry picking, sitting out on the front porch and drinking homemade lemonade until it was time to go to bed. Funny how I recall leaving the front door propped open so the cool night breeze could blow through the house. I also remember, on hot summer days, my sisters and I would entertain ourselves by turning up the radio and listening to forbidden music. The music that was forbidden was rock and roll—anything other than good, wholesome Christian music.

It was the summer of 1964, and my sister Sue and I were bored. At last, Mama and Daddy had left the house. We both knew what that meant. It was our opportunity to listen to rock and roll, play music and dance, do all the things that we had been taught were of the world and would send us to hell—well, not all the things. We dare not cuss, smoke, or drink as we wouldn't have known how to get our hands on those things anyway. We should have known better because usually it was Jean on the lookout for Mama's car, Marion who had control of the stereo, so there was always someone on look-out to pronounce, "Mama's coming!" I guess either we were being particularly brave that day or Beatlemania got the best of us, for that day our mind was not on going to hell but on the Beatles. Yes, that's right. We two little black girls in Kingston, Tennessee, were smitten by the Fab Four.

It was usually my Sister Sue who came up with the master plan, and I just followed along. This time was different. I got the bright idea to see what all those girls get out of screaming over the Beatles. With this as our goal, we went about the task at hand. First we had to close all the windows (remember, this is in the middle of summer, and we have no air-conditioner). Closing windows was central to our plan so as to not be heard. We then ventured into forbidden territory—my mother's bedroom—because not only was this where a small radio was, it had the best mirror to get a full-length view. To make matters worse, perhaps we were suffering from near heatstroke as the heat index in that little wooden house was, I'm sure, over one hundred degrees.

We began to jump and roll on our parents' bed, and to top it off, on her white George Washington bedspread. My mother's pride and joy was her new bedspread, and we had been admonished to stay off! It only took a matter of a few seconds to scan the stations to find that song we had been waiting for. Almost as if being cued, we both started screaming and rolling, even jumping, on Mama's white George Washington bedspread. Perhaps it was being in forbidden territory that made it so appealing; perhaps it was the beat of the music. In any event, we forgot our senses, or as Mama would say, "lost our ever-loving minds." We screamed and screamed and jumped and rolled around on the inviting white mound of a bed. I was only interrupted by Sue's, "Shhh. I think I hear something." We turned the radio down a bit and, after hearing nothing, continued to scream. Think that day they must have been having a Beatle marathon as it seemed the song went on and on forever.

Suddenly we thought what we heard became a reality. There was literal banging on the front door, and now I could see Daddy's face at the bedroom window with a crowbar trying to pry the window open in order to save his children. All I remember hearing him say was, "Lord have mercy, those children have been electrocuted." Without saying a word, Sue dashed out of the room and ran down the hall and jumped in bed, pretending to be asleep. She left me still stunned at the unfolding events. I was left to straighten out the bed, turn the music off, and open the door for Mama. My life seemingly flashed before me as I slowly and sheepishly went to the front door, opened it, and before I knew it, a little black arm reached inside over my head and grabbed me by the scrub of my collar (from the back side).

My daddy, still expressing concern that we had been electrocuted, was drowned out by Mama's astute revelation that "they ain't been doing nothing except screaming over dem Beatles." There may have been a feeble confession on my part, but to no avail. I remember being pushed facedown into the couch and given a whipping with a flyswatter, metal handle and all. After what seemed an eternity of a whipping, Sue emerged from the back of the house rubbing her eyes and pretending to have been asleep. I was seething mad with her because by the time Mama finished my beating, she had no more energy to whip Sue. That was a strange twist of events. Usually, I was the one that conned my way out of whippings. I would cry and scream so much because my mother was whipping my sisters that Mama usually had mercy on me and actually said one time to Daddy, "That child done screamed and holla'd, so I don't need to whip her." To this day, some fifty plus years later, hearing that song brings back bittersweet memories.

***"I'm gone "put the little pot in the big un" (on cooking)."**

"What's for Dinner?"

Aside from raising twelve chiren and starting one of the first black-owned businesses in Kingston, Tennessee, one of the things Mama was noted for was her cooking. I do not ever recall hearing the question asked, "What do you want for dinner?" Nor did we ever utter the words (at least not out loud), "I do not want or like that." Looking back on it, dinnertime in the Liggett household was a bit of an adventure. Some of her most famous delicacies were cooked up during hog-killing season. We didn't own any hogs, of course; but every fall or winter, we managed to get one from Brother Roy Stone, a young minister from Concord, Tennessee, whom my parents loved as one of their own children. Aside from the usual delicacies from the hog (i.e., chitterlings, hog snout, brain, ham, bacon, etc.), there was the occasional critter that would find its way to our table. I distinctly remember coming to eat only to be met with a charred oily-looking opossum who was laid out on the table—teeth and all—who seemed to fix his gaze on me and stared me down almost as if in a contest. It didn't help that I was at eye level with the table. My mother then instructed me, "Honey, get you some of that dark meat out the top of his head." All I remember from that dinner—for surely, I must have unconsciously repressed all memories except unfortunately for the taste of that night—is that it was oily and greasy and had the most disgusting taste. The rest of the evening was a blur.

There was also the time when my sister Sue and I were called to the table and could not wait to partake of whatever was producing that wonderful smell from the kitchen. Mama emerged from the kitchen and placed the hot steaming bowl of something in front of us and told us to dig in. We could only see that it was meat, and it was submerged in what appeared to be delicious gravy. Upon further examination—and by examination, I mean a fork poked at the floating object—we found that a huge hog's snout came bobbling to the top of the surface. We simultaneously squealed as we were convinced that the pepper that was so generously sprinkled in the gravy was boogers! After we fled the table in horror, the only thing left for my mother to do was to laugh and then give us the "ya'll don't know what's good for ya" speech.

Each new week meant the possibility of being exposed to some new part of an animal. Like the time Mama brought home a calf tongue from the Cas Walker Store. She carefully stored her treasure in the bottom of the refrigerator. What she never knew is that we would take that treasure and chase one another around the house with it. Worse, still it helped us tremendously with our chores. One of the task assigned was to lick and stick the infamous S&H Green Stamps. If you are of a certain age, you remember licking these stamps and then taking them to the S&H redemption store for an iron or a silver dish or some other treasure. When she finally came to cook it, I remember how she would rave about the taste and how tender it was. Sue and I, of course, made our excuses for not being hungry and held the snickers under our breath while Mamma and Daddy enjoyed their delicacy.

I'll whip yo behind 'til it ropes like okra.
—Ms. Naioma Walker
(Claxton, Tennessee)

I will stomp a mudhole in yo behind
and step in it and walk it dry.
—Lula Ingram
(Columbus, Georgia)

I done broke that same stick
you tryin' to walk with.
—Orlinda Gray
(Knoxville, Tennessee)

***"I'll whip yo behind as long as I can keep up with it."**

***"I wanna whip him 'til I fall out."**

***"Gal, I'll wrang my hand off in yo face."**
***"I'll slap you into the middle of next week."**
***"I'll slap the walking dog out of you."**

***"I'll pay you back for new and old."**

***"Gal, you gotta come by me."**

Got that "can't don't ya hair."
Can't comb it and don't ya try.
—Ms. Emma Coleman of Georgia

"Three Crops of Chiren"

I can't imagine the frustrations that must have come with raising twelve children. We were not all raised together. As Mama used to say, we came along like crops in a field. And just about the time she had harvested her first crop, then there would come a second and then finally her third crop. I was born a part of Mama's third and last crop. I can't imagine having twelve children, not to mention the three she obtained after she and Daddy married. Let alone raising and disciplining that many. Of course, by the time she and Daddy married, my other siblings by Daddy's first wife were grown or in college. We, like most kids, were lively and high-spirited, and I suppose at times just plain hardheaded. Mama used to tease me by saying that had she known about the pill, I—being her twelfth child—would most certainly not have been born. As a matter of fact, she proudly boasted the last three or four of her chiren wouldn't be here.

Long before the threat of child abuse loomed over my parents' head, my mother was famous for her backhand licks. In fact, she was so good at it she could get four of her kids at the same time while we were sitting in the back seat of the car (of course, this was back in the day when there were no seat belts). One thing I've noticed is that African American mothers, especially of my mother's generation, were famous for making threats that were most assuredly never carried out (due to the fact of their sheer outrageousness of course), but the mere threat of hearing one of these gems was sure to make you, as my momma often said, "straighten up and fly right." Other original gems were as follows:

"I'll slap the walking dog out of you."

"I'll slap the stew out ya mouth.

"I'll slap half your back off" (had to be the favorite because that was the go-to threat).

"I'll wrang wring my hand off in yo face."

"I'll slap the taste out yo mouth."

"I'm go'n whip you 'til I fall out."

"I'll knock fire out of you."

"I'm go'n pay you back for new and old."

"I'm go'n turn you every which way but lose."

"I'll slap the living mess out of you."

If there ever was a phrase that could send cold chills down my spine, it was the one when Mama's voice dropped a couple of octaves (as she was known to change octaves within a range of five or seven at a minute's notice). Her eyes began to dance back and forth as she uttered, "Gal, you got to come by me," which of course meant we had to walk past her as she was prone and positioned to take a swing at us.

Never at a loss for words—or rather, weapons, as we viewed it—she could produce a weapon of mass destruction from any common household item. If she could not find her weapon of choice—which was Daddy's old brown beat-up belt which used to hang on the coat rack, in full view of the children (there were several slick spots on it as it had been well seasoned by reason of use)— nonetheless, if she could not find her weapon of choice, she would always use whatever was handy: a fly swatter, a shoe, etc. Daddy would proclaim he could make the belt talk as he clapped it and said Dr. Pepper. Momma used to say she could use her house shoe, and it would serve dual purpose. She could whip the girls with the flat part of the shoe and use the heel of the shoe on the boys. Well, I never saw this because there were no boys in her last crop of chiren—only split tails—girls.

Before the beating always came the barrage of threats. This, mind you, could last for days or right before the correction. I hated it when she would put whippings in layaway (i.e., store them up). If one of us had done something belt worthy but she was tired, she would say, "You know I'm too tired to whip that gal, but I owe you one." Trust me, you would much rather she beat you on the spot as to lay it up because the day, the moment you did something and she was rested, then she would pay you back for new and old. "You know I promised that gal a whipping last week." And there you would have it—two beatings for the price of one.

The "Stored-Up" Whuppin'

After a long, hard day at the beauty shop, Mama would come home tired. We knew to have our chores done, which usually either involved ironing a basket of clothes or washing the dishes, as well as cleaning our rooms. Woe be unto us if that wasn't done. We knew not to hit her with questions or a bunch of news, for if she had promised us a whipping (which she often did if she were too tired from a long day of doing hair at the beauty salon), she would promise us one or put one in layaway, so to speak. If we were due for a whopping, we were extra careful not to do anything to remind her. Sometimes even the best-laid plans did not work, so we knew to be prepared.

When the barrage of threats became real and we knew our punishment was imminent, we did the only thing we could do (i.e., prepare). It was Sue's bright idea to pad ourselves in preparation for the beating. Like soldiers getting ready for battle, we rummaged through drawers and clothes hampers to obtain rags, clothes, towels, anything we could find to absorb the belt. Now you have to understand, Sue weighed all of sixty pounds or less throughout elementary school. After the padding, she looked like a little chubby, fat kid who might have flown under the radar had she not giggled when the belt was applied. Perhaps if she had have feigned tears, but since she did not, Mama immediately started removing the padding. And once all extra articles were removed, she would start over.

One might expect that after receiving a whipping—deserved or not—tears would likely follow. I never could understand the logic behind this. Once my mother would give us what she would call a "half-killing," she would dare us to cry. "Gal, you better dry it up, or I'll give you something to cry about." No, thank you, Mama. You just did, and that's why I'm crying.

I'll knock yo jawbone straddle yo throat.
—Orlinda Grey
(Knoxville, Tennessee)

Child's hair looks like "Wootietoot" (Nappy).

—Ms. Annie Campbell (Bristol, Tennessee)

***"I'll slice you too thin to fry."**

***"Honey, git all you can and can all you can git" (about education).**

Every shut-eye ain't sleep, and every good-bye ain't gone.

***"Don't act yo color."**
***"Don't show yo behind."**
***"Don't act a monkey."**

The White Lady Told Me to Do It

In Greenwood Elementary School, or the colored school (as it was called), there were many things we could do but many we could not. Among those we could not do was to interrupt our teacher or act out or misbehave in any way while the *white lady* was visiting. I do not remember her name, but I will never forget the excitement and how all the kids were abuzz with the news that the white lady was coming tomorrow! When the white lady came, she would always introduce us to some new delicacy or wonder that surely little colored children in Kingston had never ever seen. One time, she brought in a pet rabbit for those of us brave enough to pet it. One time it was seashells. Surely, none of us had ever seen the ocean in person; but when we held those big shells up to ours ears, we certainly could hear the ocean, and some imagined they could feel the ocean spray.

One day, before the arrival of the white lady, all the kids were sent outside for an extended recess. Before being sent outside, we were, in essence, read our rights. We knew that, above all things, you should never act out in front of the white lady. You look your best; you remember to wear your best clothes and to iron the ribbon in your hair; and above all, you never come inside while the teacher was speaking to the white lady. Why oh why did I, quiet shy little Joy, violate both rules on the same day and at the same time? If there is one lesson that was drilled into the minds of little black children in the 1950s, it was know how to behave in front of white folks, or as Mamma often said—don't act yo color.

I don't remember what the argument was about, but I got in an argument with one of my best friends Marilyn W. Apparently, someone told Marilyn that I had made Kathy H. cry again. The details have become murky over the years. Marilyn proclaimed, "I believe it." For some reason, I was so incensed that my good name had been besmirched; and almost without a thought, I proceeded to march up the stairs and into the school house. Almost like an out-of-body experience, I continued to march up the stairs amidst unheeded warning cries of, "Don't go in there, Joy. You know that white lady is in there." I pushed the door open and marched up to my beloved Miss Gertrude (who oddly enough did not have kind eyes toward me but a frown). Without a thought, I blurted out, "Ms. Gertrude, Marilyn said that I said —— about Kathy…and I didn't."

Had this been one of those made-for-TV movies, right about now the action would be cued for slow motion, and there would be the obligatory slurred shouts of, "Nooo. Get outta there." The white lady turned to me and said (to all of our shock), "Well, you just go out there and give her a sock." Having been given the ultimate free pass, I started winding up my arm, fist formed, and promptly marched—no, stomped—outside. Almost without being able to see straight, I spotted Marilyn through the blur of my rage. "I'm go'n git you. I'm go'n git you. I'm go'n git you," was all I could seem to get out. Marilyn stood stoic but surprised and never fought back as I slapped, hit, and screamed at her. I distinctly remember picking rocks up and throwing them on her new patent leather shoes and taking a stick and picking her tights. Looking back, I am so ashamed of my actions. I had never been in a fight in my entire life—before or since. Well, except with my sisters. And then there was that one time that my sister Sue and I (along with the Hamilton sisters) rocked Donald S. and took his bike for repeatedly riding by our house and calling us the *N* word. But other than that, I had never been in a fight in my life.

Blinded by what felt like a righteous carte blanche to fight, I did not hear the crowds yelling and was not aware of when my sister Marion came out of Mr. Powell's room to come (not to my aid) to the aid of a crying Marilyn. She took her in the bathroom and washed her face. What no one questioned at the time was the fact that I did not get in trouble with Miss Gertrude for fighting. Any other time, a paddling would have been swift and deliberate. When asked by those standing around who witnessed the carnage why she didn't paddle me, Miss Gertrude simply said she decided not to paddle me because the white lady had told me to do it.

When I got home, Marilyn's mother called my mother to tell her that she whupped Marilyn for fighting (even though Marilyn never even tried to defend herself) and admonished Mama to whup me too. I remember sitting outside on the front porch, pulling my breath in and listening to Mama talk on the phone to Marilyn's mother. Even though I was outside, I could still hear Mama clearly as she talked very loudly. I heard the words that both pleased and surprised me: "I'm not go'n whip Joy 'cause that white lady told her to fight." What lesson I must have learned that day. The words of the white lady were very powerful.

***"He's so short you could lick salt off the top of his head."**

***"If it was raining soup,
you'd have a fork."**

The Day the Schools Integrated

History was made in September of 1964 as about twelve or so black children integrated the Roane County School System. It was because of Mama and Helen Hamilton, or Miss Helen as we had to call her, that the schools integrated in the first place. If you were to ask her if she were an activist, she would say no but for some reason can't totally remember why she was on a crutch. Something to do with a bone in her foot pulling lose (funny, I have that same extra bone), and apparently Miss Helen had broken her foot. As the story goes (real, not folklore), she and Miss Helen decided to pay the superintendent of Roane County Schools a visit as the account goes both without invitation nor appointment. When they got there, pushing past the objections of the secretary, they asked why the schools in Kingston had not integrated yet. As they gave him the third degree—which involved loud talking and shaking the crutch in the face of the superintendent—he reluctantly agreed. In the school year of 1964–1965, Kingston Schools were integrated.

I was nine years old and would be one of the few to integrate Kingston Elementary School. There would be only me and one other girl, Marilyn Woods, who would be in my fifth grade class. I will never forget the walk to school nor the clothes I had on that day. The night before, I had plenty of anxiety. Yes, going to the white school was good 'cause of angst, but Mama had made sure that I looked my best. Albeit being a beautician, she had taken great care to make sure my hair was washed and pressed and that I had on good school clothes. I still remember what I had on—I wore a new blue and white gingham dress with brown oxfords and white ankle socks. My hair was in three braids or plaits (as we called them), and I had a blue bow on my top braid. The bow was an essential accessory that had become a part of me since the days in the colored school, as it was called. When you forgot your bow, you had to sit in a special chair away from the rest of the class as punishment. I both loved and hated those bows. I loved the feel and look of a freshly tied bow that had been carefully ironed and laid out the night before. I did not like the fact that if I forgot it, I would be punished by Miss Gertrude and made fun of by my classmates. I was ready and both excited and petrified of being black in a white school, but on top of that, it had been late when Mama got in from the beauty shop, and she did not have time to buy me a notebook. Believe it or not, this caused me the most anxiety.

Being one of few black people in a sea of white faces, and on top of that, no notebook. Having had children of my own, I cannot imagine what it would be like to send my little sixty-pound (wringing-wet) girl into that situation. It makes me have even more respect for her. I remember the walk up the hill from my house to the white school took all of five minutes, but it seemed like an eternity. I never would have been caught out in public holding Mama's hand, but that day, I held on for dear life. I will always remember the look of determination in her eye and the way my little brown hand became lost in her larger slightly calloused black hand. She tightened the grip and walked straight on. I do not recall any conversation, but I do remember her lips silently moving as we headed up that hill. I now know she was praying. We finally reached the front door and went up about seven or eight steps. We then took a right turn, and there was another set of seven or eight steps this time that led downward into the main hallway where fifth and sixth grade classrooms were.

And then we saw and heard it: a literal sea of white faces and all the noises that come with the first day of classes. Mothers with their children holding on to pieces of paper and suddenly announcing, "Here's your room." There were hugs and tears as parents dropped their students off at their respective classrooms. In the midst of the roar and din of this crowd, all of a sudden there was complete silence. Strange that the silence happened as soon as we appeared at the top of the stairs. I suddenly felt the grip on my hand tighten and heard a strange tone to Mama's voice that appeared to be not fear but perhaps apprehension. I never thought about what was going through my mother's mind, but all I know was, she must have been a brave woman. The only words spoken were, "Let's go," as her grip became almost a pull as she led me down the stairs and through the crowd. We did not have to worry about accidentally bumping into people as the crowd parted like the Red Sea. All I could do was to pray, not in the same way that Mama prayed, I'm sure. My prayer was simply, "God, please don't let anyone call us that word. Of course, at that time—long before it became politically incorrect and dubbed the *N* word—the word *nigger* was a way of life for us.

If someone said it, I never heard it because before I knew it, we were at Mrs. Hale's classroom. Mama again spoke, "Here's your room." She gave me a gentle push into the room and said simultaneously, "You'll be fine." I didn't feel fine as Mrs. Hale was nowhere to be seen. She and her desk was surrounded by eager faces all wanting to make themselves known. I just stood motionless in the front of the classroom—too afraid to move, too afraid to be seated—for I fear that I would sit in a seat already taken by a white person and too embarrassed not to because I was black and because I had no notebook.

I have often wondered what it was like for Mama as she made her way back through the crowds and walked home. What was it like for her to wonder how her baby fared that day? Well, her baby did just fine. Before I could worry any longer, a student named Laverne Holbrook came up to me and introduced herself and invited me to sit beside her. Much to my surprise and delight, my good friend Marilyn (from the colored school) was also seated nearby. We both sighed a sigh of relief and settled in our seats, being careful not to mess up our freshly pressed outfits or hair. One simple check—and yes, we both wore our hair ribbons. Marilyn's was red, and I wore a blue one to match my outfit. Even though we were no longer in the colored school and Miss Gertrude was no longer our teacher, we (I'm convinced) did it for her. Plus, we learned our lesson well on how to behave and look when in front of the white folks.

The Sixth Grade Dance

Few lessons in life stay with you, like the one Mama taught us at a young age. I am sure she had to learn it for self-preservation, but if I heard it once, I heard it a thousand times: the proverbial admonitions for behavior around white people. One of the earliest lessons I learned from Miss Mamie. I knew if I could learn this one lesson and get it right, then I would be accepted. At the end of my second year of being in the white school, it was the summer of 1966. In spite of everything else that was going on—the war in Vietnam, the emergence of the miniskirt—that summer marked the second year in the white school and the first time a party was to be given for all junior high–bound sixth graders. Although it has been some years since that time, it only takes a few seconds in my mind, and I am immediately transported back to my hometown of Kingston.

I suppose in many ways my coming of age was similar to that of most eleven-year-olds. I looked forward to going to junior high in the fall and secretly longed to get my period before becoming a teenager. I fussed with my hair and wanted to make sure the pleats in my dress were ironed just right. I listened to the Beatles on the radio when I could—that was usually when Mama and Daddy would leave the house. My parents, you see, had early pronounced them to be long-haired hippies who played the devil's music. I would nonetheless slip into their bedroom and listen; it was there I found the best mirror in the house. It gave me a view from head to toe, and this was important when practicing the latest dance steps.

The party for six graders was announced over the intercom at school. This in itself made us feel special. We were the envy of the school. Not only were we leaving elementary school and going to junior high, but there was a party to be given in our honor at the local community center. There was much work to be done before the party. There was a dress to buy, my hair to be done, which for me meant to be washed and pressed. I did not want it fixed too close to the party because I did not want it to look greasy. I always hated it when I would come to school after getting my hair done, and one of the white kids would put their hands in my hair and retrieve, in my estimation, enough grease to fry a chicken. On the other hand, I didn't want it to be done too far away from the party, for I feared I would sweat it back, and it might look nappy and feel like—as one of the white children said who felt my hair—cotton candy. I wanted it to be just right. I wanted it to bounce like the white girls when I did the pony.

It seemed as if an eternity had passed, but the night of the party finally arrived. I must admit, I felt a little like Cinderella getting ready for the ball. In this case, I would not be arriving in a carriage drawn by six white horses who had been mice in a previous life, but I would walk to the party flanked by my three sisters behind me, giving last-minute tips on what to do and how to act. I knew if I could just remember everything they taught me, I would be fine.

I arrived at the Kingston Community Center and either mustered the courage to walk through the door or was pushed by one of my sisters; I cannot remember which. In any event, I found myself inside. It was strange. I didn't feel particularly colored (as we were called in the summer of 1966) that night. What I did feel was grown-up and a bit nervous. I was nervous at the prospect of a boy asking me to dance and even more nervous at the prospect of nobody asking me to dance. It was my first party with boys—who am I kidding?—my first party ever (unless you count the birthday party that Sue had been invited to by one of the boys from the colored school when I was about six). I got to tag along even though I had not been officially invited. I was the baby and cried and sulked until Mama asked if I could tag along. Sue was not happy with that decision.

As I entered the door and saw all of my classmates, my eyes quickly scanned the room desperately, seeking a seat so that I could quickly sit down and blend in. Even before I was finished scanning, I was greeted by a rather soft-spoken lady with a nervous smile, who gently but firmly placed her hands on my shoulders and turned me around and guided me toward the door. She simply said, "I don't think you're supposed to be here tonight. I think there's another night for you to come." I tried to explain to her that, yes, tonight was the night. All my classmates were there. My friend Leslie, whom I had spoken to on the phone and giggled with about liking the same boy, was there. Before I could manage to get more than a few mutters out of my mouth and make eye contact with Leslie in a plea for help, I was ushered out of the door.

The time it had taken me to walk in and then be escorted out must have taken a matter of seconds. My sisters were still outside the door, looking just as puzzled as I must have looked when I merged. They asked me what had happened, and I explained to them what the soft-spoken lady with the nervous smile had said. Needless to say, the walk home was extremely quiet. The quiet was interrupted only by the well-meaning attempts of my sisters to cheer me up. "You didn't want to go to that old dance anyway," one sister said. To this day, my sister BJ continues to be one of my biggest cheerleaders. Another one said, "Those people are just prejudice." I am not recalling her exact words, nor the sister from whom it came (I suspect it was my sister Sue), but I believe there was judgement passed on the woman, her children, and upon all of those who attended the party. Something to the effect of, "That ole building ought to burn down"; and when she dies (referring to the soft-spoken lady with the nervous smile), she's probably going straight to hell. All I clearly remember on that walk home is that it seemed to take much longer going than coming.

In my mind, I tried to make some sense out of what had just transpired, but I simply did not comprehend what had happened back at that community center. I had followed all the rules; I had done exactly as I had been taught. Mama and my sisters had taught me well the lessons of life: how to sit, how to speak, and how not to stand out and call attention to myself. Above all, they had taught me how to act in front of the white people. In other words, I had been well versed in the art of how not to act my color. On that day, it did not matter; and for the second time (the first time was the first day of school in the white school), I felt colored, really colored. I nevertheless proudly put one foot with its Vaseline-shined patent leather shoe in front of the other, choking back tears until I was home. When I walked through the door, I quickly went to the back and carefully hung up my dress. Mama didn't really ask a lot of questions. I think she could tell by my face and the face of my sisters what had happened. Once the story was relayed, she too uttered something about the future of that woman's soul and her place in eternity.

I Wanna Smoke Like Miss Mer (Mary) Kate

Before Miss Mamie opened up Liggett's Salon, one of the first black-owned business in Kingston, she would do hair on the back porch of the house. Sometimes Sue and I would wait with customers in the living room. And sometimes we would be summoned to the back porch by a customer who wanted to see us or by Mama who wanted a drink of water or to pick something up off the floor that she had dropped. You do know that back in the day, we were the remote control. I so remember even while in college, I would be in the back bedroom studying for an important exam, only to be called to the front of the house to change the television station on a television that was less than five feet away from either parent, but that's another story.

Two main things stand out in my mind about Mama's shop on the back porch. Number one was Ms. Mer Kate. Her actual name was Mary Kate, but the people in Kingston (including my family) slurred her name all together. What can I say about Ms. Mer Kate? Two things immediately come to mind and that I knew for sure about her. Number one, she was hell bound. She wore bloodred nail polish, drunk, and boy, she sure could smoke a cigarette. How did I know she was going to hell? My father was a Church of God preacher; and anyone who smoked, cussed, drank, wore red lipstick was on their way to hell. Well, Ms. Mer Kate had excelled in each category.

I remember one time hearing about how her family (could have been her sons) found her drunk and naked in a ditch. What I remember the most—well, to be completely truthful, what I admired the most—about Miss Mer Kate was the way she smoked a cigarette. Smoking was not allowed in our house, but somehow Mama made an exception for her customers as they could smoke in the Knoxville or big-city beauty shops. I remember one summer day Sue and I would sit together on the steps of the back porch and watch Miss Mer Kate smoke her cigarette. The way she took her hands with that bloodred fingernail polish and tapped out a cigarette was simply mesmerizing. She placed the cigarette and balanced it between her lips as she continued to carry on a conversation with our mother. *How can she do that*, I thought, *without it falling?* She never lost the cigarette nor missed a beat talking. Next came the best part: she lit the dangling object and drew the fiery smoke in. Boy, the way she'd hold that cigarette with those red nails and the way she pulled that smoke in like it was the best thing ever was almost hypnotic. But then something almost magical happened. While still talking, she released the smoke through her nose. My sister and I later agreed that when we grew up, we wanted to smoke just like Miss Mer Kate. My sister did take up smoking as a brief experiment and test to her womanhood when she went to college, but I never have smoked a cigarette to this day. Initially, I did not do it because I did not want to be hell-bound like Miss Mer Kate. Now because they stink, and I know how harmful they can be to one's health. Have you ever kissed someone who smokes? Don't! It truly is like kissing an ashtray!

The Day I Ruined Christmas

"Honey, That's Just an Ole White Man with a Beard"

What can I say about that day? It was like any other school day, but for many, it would be life altering. Before the schools integrated, I had to be around seven or eight years of age and in the second or third grade (could have been the fourth). In any event, grades one to four were in one room—Ms. Gertrude's room—and five to eight were in Mr. Powell's room. To my recollection, it was warm weather, which makes my actions even harder to explain. As the custom at Greenwood Elementary, each grade of about seven or eight students would form a circle, and then our teacher would float from grade to grade teaching the lesson for the day. Greenwood—or the colored school, as we were referred to in the community—was a two-room schoolhouse with wooden floors, whose oily smell mixed with the acrid smell of burning cinders in the furnace room would greet students as we filed in.

Gertrude Porter or Miz Gertrude or Miz Gerrrrtruuuude (when we wanted her to come by). We sat in anticipation, working on our lesson, as Miz Gertrude floated from grade to grade. She would often start with the first graders. Once finished with them, she gave them an assignment to work on or simply had them rest their heads on their desk until she went to the next grade. Little Vaseline-shined legs would wiggle and kick up and down, and hands would be raised anxious for our turn as we sang the song of accomplishment: "Miss Gertrude, come by," "Miss Gertrude, come by," "I know my lesson," "I know my lesson."

Maybe I wanted attention; or maybe "Ms. Gertrue," as we slurred her name, was taking too long in getting to us. I distinctly remember raising my hand (this was our way of getting the teacher's attention or asking a question). Hands raised high, I was recognized by Miss Gertrude. "Yes, Joy."

I did not have a question but rather wanted to make a statement. I proudly proclaimed, "My daddy's a preacher."

"Yes, Joy, we know," said Ms. Gertrude with almost a head shake as if to say, *Why is she telling us this?* A few seconds went by, and my hand shot up again. "Preachers don't lie."

"Yes, Joy, I know," this time a little aggravated.

A few more seconds went by. My hand shot up the third time, and almost without being recognized, I blurted it out, "MY DADDY SAY'S THERE'S NO SUCH THING AS SANTA CLAUS!"

There was about a two-second hush and then the audible sobbing, and tears started. The tears and sobs came primarily from the first graders. Some had to be carried out and have their faces washed. Others were too upset to continue the day, and parents were called to come get them. Then Miss Gertrude angrily scolded me, "You and your big mouth."

I turned with a smirk and went about my work, convinced that I had set the world straight. My friends in my grade asked me if that's true, what about the Santa Claus in the parades? My comeback was what Mama always told me, "That's just some ole white man wearing a suit and a beard." I look back on that day and still do not know what I was thinking or what was my purpose in crushing the dreams of little black girls and boys on that day.

Yo head might a growed up in
the clouds, but your *ass* stayed
down here low where I am!
—Ms. Louise M. Underwood
(courtesy of Ronni Chandler)

***"A hard head makes a soft behind."**
"The more you cry, the less you'll pee."
—L. Brown

***"You ain't got cornbread sense."**

***"He's so ugly look like his head done wo' (wore) out two or three bodies."**

***"Hair 'bout close to her head as ninety-nine is to one hundred."**

***"It's a po' (poor) dog that won't wag his own tail."**

***"The devil will put a pound of sugar on a pickle."**

—Baby Cherlye

*"If you can't push a pencil—you sho dog can push a plow."

"Child looks like corn bread
'bout the head"
—Gilbert Liggett

"I'm so tired, I'm propped up on every leaning side."

—O. Grey
(Knoxville, Tennessee)

"A new broom sweeps clean, but an old one knows the corners."

—F. King
(Oregon)

"Keep yo eyes open and yo mouth shut."

"A new broom may sweep clean, but an old one starts leaving dust."

—E. Hall (Memphis, Tennessee)

***"I hope he went where I think he didn't" (in speculation of whether or not someone went to heaven).**

I had a fit and fell back in it.

—Charlotte Ingram
(Columbus, Georgia)

***"Sit on yo fist and rare back on yo thumb."**

***"The blacker the berry, the sweeter the juice."**

**You make corn bread for your husband,
but you make biscuits for your man.**

**—Ercille Hall
(Memphis, Tennessee)**

*"Fix Yo Face"

First of all, Miss Mamie would say in her Southern Georgia drawl, "Honey, fix yo face." Okay, by this, did she mean put on makeup? Surely not. Because her husband, my daddy, the Reverend Orange Gilbert Liggett, frowned upon and even preached from the pulpit against makeup and the perils of those painted ladies. At one time during a sermon, a lady on the front with scarlet-red lipstick was so pointed out as on her way to hell for wearing such. All I remember is that she quickly retreated from the front row and left the church in a huff. No one went after her. No one was concerned about losing members, only preaching the Gospel. My daddy's favorite phrase (one effectively used to chase Jehovah Witnesses away, I might add) was, "I hope you see the error of your way before it's finally everlasting too late and you burn in a devil's hell."

So what did she mean? She explained to me as I was pursuing my second career and studying to be a nurse. She said one day while lying the bed, "Now, Joy, you go'n have patients who is sick. They may not smell good. Some of 'em may be fat." In case you are wondering, Miss Mamie was not politically correct. She called it exactly like she saw it. You weren't plump or big-boned; you were fat. You didn't have a bad odor; you stunk. She was known to tell you to your face, so you definitely had to have your big-girl panties on if you ever got to be in Miss Mamie's presence. She continued, "Now when you go into they room, don't be all frowned up. You go'n smell things you ain't never smelled before, but remember dey's sick. You don't want them to feel bad about themselves."

I can't tell you how many times as a nurse I have had to draw on that one. I remember during my first year of nursing I had a patient who weighed over six hundred pounds. Now we were given med lists or MARs, as they were called, as we hadn't started paper charting. Oftentimes, even without knowing the diagnosis, you can tell what is wrong with a patient by looking at their med lists. You can imagine upon looking at this particular patient's list, my heart sunk. As I say two medicines, they were both creams with the instructions, on one, apply to folds; and the instructions on the other, apply in the creases. Before I walked in the room, Miss Mamie's words floated into my head as I knocked. "Fix yo face. Fix yo face." Nothing could have prepared me for the sight I was about to see: the largest yet most pleasant young man I had ever encountered. He was on a specialty bed (off the record, the nurses referred to them as big-boy beds). He was completely naked with a sheet across his midsection, which would be tossed to the side in a minute without warning.

I mustered up all the professionalism that I could as I proceeded to apply the first application of cream to the folds on the front side. The task was daunting as I tried to calculate in my head (all while fixing my face) just how to go about this. Should I put a dab on my gloved finger and apply like I would my makeup? No, that would take too long. I applied a strip of ointment to the side of my hand, and I would, in one smooth stroke, apply the cream under his breasts. This was the most non-self-conscious man that I had ever encountered in this situation. What am I saying? I had never encountered anyone in this situation.

As the patient tried to oblige me and help by lifting his large flap that included his breast so I could go about my task, he let the fat roll slip; and not only did it grab and engulf my hand but my entire arm. All I kept thinking as I felt the hot and gritty appendage weighing heavy on my arm, Don't scream. Don't shriek. Fix your face, fix yo face. I somehow managed to pry my arm loose from the blob of flesh that engulfed it and finished my task. It took me a full forty-five minutes to apply cream to the folds just on the front of this man. Even with his help, it was so difficult to move large flaps and folds to apply cream only to find leftover smelly cream from the day or days before. This particular young man was so overweight that he had to walk with the help of a cane. The cane proved to be of particular assistance when it came to placing the ointment in his groin area. The man had to lift his scrotum, or as he called it "his goober," with his cane so I could get to places I needed to. I was sweating and had other patients I had to attend to. That was the truth. But the real truth was, I needed a mental-health break. I didn't want to let it show in my face that all I ever really wanted to do was to sit in a corner and suck my thumb or go into a fetal position.

I came back at a later time to cream his backside. Dear Lord, I prayed, how in the world would I even get to his backside? As I gathered my thoughts and fixed my face, I knocked on the door and hear a gleeful "Come on in." To my surprise and private delight, I found my patient sitting in a chair and waiting to be creamed on his backside. I wasn't prepared for what happened next. He stood up and bent over to show me his butt and asked, was anything bleeding? I noticed a small amount of blood when he got up and also a small skin tear. As nurses, we constantly have to be on the lookout for pressure ulcers, and it is a matter of routine to check the patient's backside. The fact that he was already out of bed and mobile enough to show it to me was, as some might say, a gift from the gods. This creaming went much smoother, and I managed to get out of the room within about fifteen to twenty minutes—but not before being offered to partake from his arsenal of goodies (i.e., skittles, cotton candy, bubble gum, and honey buns). As a matter of fact, his fiancée and father were both eating honey buns, and all three were watching the Food Channel. I could say so much more here, but once again, "Fix yo face, Joy."

Yon, My Baby

In my mother's eyes, the most important job that anyone could ever do is to be a teacher. I can't tell you how proud she was when I first started teaching on the college level. She would come to each graduation to watch me march in with the faculty processional. I tried to explain to her that I was not getting a degree, but nevertheless, not only would she come but she would invite relatives to see me march. One year, there was my uncle Lyndsey or my brother Thomas that I hadn't seen in years. She always knew the date of the Roane State Graduation in spite of my feeble attempts to throw her off the track. The moment of truth finally came when I would march in adorned in my regalia. Before my row of faculty was seated, I heard the familiar sound, "That's my baby," which in her Georgia accent sounded more like, "Dat's my baby." As if almost on cue, I would spot her big hat and all in the crowds grinning from ear to ear and pointing, satisfied that she had spotted me.

Miss Mamie was both known for her cooking as well as her large hats. She would often show us girls how to wear it. She would say, "Now this is how you wear it. You got to break it down and wear it over one eye." That's what wearing it mean. This wasn't the end of her yearly ritual as she would always find the president of the college and grab his hand and tell him, "I just wanna thank you for giving my child a job." Again, this would be every year for the ten years that I worked at that community college. What seemed embarrassing to me then is now a sweet memory and a true testament to the fact that to my mother being a teacher was the most important job that anyone could ever do. The fact that she was proud is an understatement.

Louie 32

Somehow, not really sure when, but Mama got a gun. Her cousin/friend Lillie, whom my mother acted as caregiver for, gave her several items from her home in exchange for taking care of her. One of those items was a gun. The fact that Mama had a gun was, at that time, not a cause for concern or alarm. We grew up with a gun in the house. Granted, it was my father's unloaded hunting gun that he kept behind the door when he went out look for squirrels and occasionally cleaned, cocked, and pointed it at our would-be suitors.

Upon any given visit, Miss Mamie was known to show us how she could load and would often twirl the gun. I remember an incident when my sister Sue and her girls were visiting. She relayed how Mama would often send her and her four girls running for cover as she came around the corner twirling her prize possession that she had named Louie 32 after its caliber.

My mother and father lived in their home together for over fifty years and never had anyone attempted to break in that house. Maybe it was the sign of the times, or maybe it was the fact that preachers were revered and respected. This all changed one day when one of Mama's former Sunday school pupils broke into her home. She returned to our little house one day to find a missing television and several pieces of jewelry missing (mainly rings that belonged to Lillie). Without any concrete proof, Mama immediately suspected Curtis and called the police to inform them who had done this deed. She somehow convinced the police to go to either his house or his sister's house, and they would find the items. They found the television in a field in the back of the house. Apparently, she must have returned to the house too quickly, and he had only had a chance to stash the television.

What was amazing is the police went to the home of the relative who was wearing a piece of stolen jewelry. Curtis was arrested, but I'm not sure if he did any time for that crime. I do know that he was in and out of jail and, at one of his out times, was rumored to have stolen the mayor's car. Shortly after one of his releases, he would walk to town or to the store, and his path of travel would take him in front of Mama's house. She would stand in the door as he passed by and shout out to him, "I bet you, you bet' not break in this house no mo' 'cause I got something for you."

Curtis, I truly believe, did not want any more trouble and, quite frankly, was probably afraid of that little black woman, and rightly so. He even went as far as telling the police about Ms. Liggett's threats. The police informed my mother that he wasn't breaking the law and had a right to walk down the street. She told them, "Well, I got something for him, and if he won't stop in the name of the law, he sho dog go'n stop in the name of Louie 32."

They said, "Now, Ms. Liggett, you can't shoot someone unless they have at least one foot in your door."

Her response was simply, "Honey, you needed worry. By the time y'all get here, I would have done shot him and drug both feet in the do'."

Curtis found a new route for his walks to town.

Mama's Hands

It's funny the things you remember most about a person after they are gone. With Mama, it was her hands. She always hid her hands and said she thought they were ugly and looked like man's hands. She never wore rings because being in the Church of God (at least the one Daddy pastored), wearing jewelry was a sin and frowned upon as being worldly. Those hands that plaited our hair as we sat on the side of the bed in the morning. Those hands that carefully pressed and tied our ribbons in our hair. Those same hands that grabbed an unsuspecting strolling chicken and wrung its neck, that shot a gun, that fried heads (pressed with a hot comb) on a Saturday night so that we would look our best in our Easter Crinkling. Those same hands that grabbed Daddy's belt and gave you one of her famous half-killings. Those same hands that felt your head and gave you such comfort when you had a fever or held your head up over the toilet as you were throwing up. Those hands who could beat out a tune on the tambourine at church, cook up—as her spiritual son Roy Stone would say—"a good ole pot a something." Those hands that made it a point to almost ritualistically mash or feel every one of her friends or family that had died. Maybe it was her way of saying goodbye or seeing if they were really dead, but it gave me great discomfort to stand by her side and see her take her black hand and mash one of her former "customs" (customers) across the chest and say, "She look just like herself"; or, in the case of one of my daddy's cousins, take out a handkerchief and spit on it to wipe the corner of his mouth because she thought they had used too much embalming fluid.

It was also those hands that would give you two limp and uninterested fingers to shake if she did not like you or if it was apparent that she wanted to send the message that you were too short to be dating one of her daughters. I specifically remember bringing a guy named Greg home to meet her. I didn't particularly like him, other than for a friend; but because I could, in her words "lick salt off the top of his head," she gave him the two limp fingers and a curt, "How do" (How do you do?) and turned and went on to other things. I was mortified because the slight was obvious. I made some kind of feeble excuse, but then after, I got ready to leave and say goodbye. She said, "Bye, baby" to me and a rather flat, "Bye, Paul" to Greg. After being reminded that his name wasn't Paul, she shrugged and simply said, "Well, he look like a Paul." That was that; she had no further use for him.

She made it very clear to us girls that because we were short, she did not want us marrying short guys, apparently not liking them either. She pulled the same limp-finger routine when my sister Sue brought again a friend home named Eugene. Eugene was white, rail thin, and stuttered when he was nervous. He had a major crush on my sister Sue, so the stuttering was even more pronounced, especially when given the two limp fingers, the obligatory salutation of "How do?" and followed by, "Nice to meet you, Paul." Again, after being told that his name was Eugene, she shrugged her shoulders and simply said, "Well, you look like a Paul." Unlike Greg, Eugene had been forewarned by Sue that Mama would not like him if he presented himself as someone who liked her daughter. I'm not so sure if it was because he was white (something that could get people of her generation killed [i.e., dating across racial lines]) or because he was again, as she put it, "right wormy-looking." This phrase was reserved for anyone who did not have a lot of muscles and could pass as a ninety-pound weakling.

All these memories washed over me as I saw her lying in the casket up front at Kyker Funeral Home in Kingston. This time, those hands were carefully laid across her belly and her nails manicured a pretty Pepto Bismol pink. This lady who never wore rings or fingernail polish had made the decision at the rehab center two weeks before her death to get her nails painted. Little did she know that her new polish would go perfect with the beautiful pink dress we picked out for her.

The day she was laid to rest, it was overcast and had intermittent rain. The one thing I remember was being in the funeral procession and seeing that big red fire truck that used to be housed at the city hall, right up the street from her house, pull across Kentucky Street, blocking traffic so the funeral procession could make its way to the graveyard.

Yes, Miss Mamie could not have planned it any better. She went home in style. No surgery, no radiation, no chemo (only a little Tylenol), and so she was laid to rest just like she had fought every battle in her life—her way and on her terms.

Childhood Home

Miss Mamie visiting Cousin Lillie in the nursing home. Took her a cake for her 90th birthday

Miss Mamie modeling one of her many
"Sunday go to meeting hats" Age 92

Miss Mamie worked as a maid before she went
to beauty school. This was taken (year unknown)
on the patio of one of those families.

Miss Mamie (and one of her classmates) posing in front of our old Buick. Taken after her graduation from beauty school @1959

Miss Mamie and one of her many babies
that she cared for (year unknown)

Mama "Miss Mamie" and Daddy "Reverend Liggett"

From Left to right Sisters Sue, Marion and me.

Joy (me) and Sue @1959

ABOUT THE AUTHOR

Joy E. Ingram was born in the small town of Kingston, Tennessee, to Reverend O. G. Liggett and Ms. Mamie Floyd (Tate) Liggett. Although both parents had a profound impact upon Joy's life, she attributes her sense of humor and strong work ethic to her fiery, God-fearing, straight-talking Georgia-bred mother. Joy has often remarked she had the fear of Miss Mamie long before she developed the fear of God. Joy started her education in a two-room segregated schoolhouse known as Greenwood Elementary School. She would not attend schools with white children until she entered the fifth grade. In spite of her markedly inferior educational beginnings, Joy would go on to receive her associate's degree from Roane State Community College in Harriman, Tennessee, and her bachelor's and master's degrees in history from the University of Tennessee, Knoxville. Joy would go back to school while teaching full-time and receive her nursing degree. In January of 2015, Joy retired from Pellissippi State as an associate professor of history after thirty-two successful years of teaching at both Roane State and Pellissippi State. Joy currently works as a registered nurse at Parkwest Medical Center in Knoxville, Tennessee. She is the mother of two grown children, Michelle and Aaron. She currently resides in Knoxville, Tennessee, with her husband, Anthony, and dog, Boaz. Writing and public speaking are two of Joy's passions.

CPSIA information can be obtained
at www.ICGtesting.com
Printed in the USA
LVHW071642071122
732483LV00031B/237/J